Made in United States
Troutdale, OR
11/13/2023

14517401R00070